20 THINGS YOU WON'T LEARN IN COLLEGE
(But REALLY Need To Know)

Kurt McDowell

First Printing August 2007
ISBN 978-1-4357-0649-1

Cover Design by *KMGraphics*

To Camden & Zoe

Table of Contents

BUSINESS

Introduction

Have you ever found an answer to a problem and wished you would have figured it out five years ago, ten years ago? The only thing wrong with learning by experience is having to wade through the experience to get there. Here in the 21st century, doggone it; we need the answers a little sooner.

When I turned 40 years old, I thought it might be a good idea to write down some key principles (let's call them "Aha!" moments) I've learned over time. These "Aha!" moments have been assembled into the principles of this book. All of these lessons I wished I would have learned sooner, and that's why I'm writing this book for the high school and college aged student. You are about to read the *CliffsNotes* of life.

This manuscript is actually a letter to *me* at 18 years of age. Maybe you resemble the guy I was 20 years ago, looking for answers but a little unsure of the questions. A Chinese proverb once stated that a smart man learns from his mistakes, but a *wise* man can learn from the mistakes of others. Hopefully you, the Reader, can benefit from *my* life experiences and from those people who have influenced me.

This book is divided in two parts – the first dealing with personal principles, the second dealing with business and professional principles. The common thread throughout is the interaction with people. The inescapable fact of life is that we have to deal with people both socially and in the business world. Identifying and understanding the rules of engagement are 70% of the battle. I hold all the tenets of this book as absolute truths, but will let you be the judge. You have embarked on an incredible journey. Cherish every moment!

KM

P.S. The title of this book should in no way dissuade anyone from gaining a college education. The author merely implies that many lessons, unfortunately, can only be gained through life experience.

PERSONAL

1
Every action has a consequence

I'm not here to insult your intelligence, but we've got to set *some* ground rules for human behavior. Life does not happen in a vacuum. Every action (or lack of action) has a consequence, whether intended or not. I'm sure you learned in science class about every action having a reaction. Well, the same principle applies here. And just like science class, the "reaction" is never neutral. It will be a either a positive consequence or a negative one.

Too often we read news stories about famous athletes, politicians or the everyman, who can't believe that their behavior has led to punitive action or public outcry. As a society, we are constantly bombarded by the message to do what feels good without a care to its repercussions. Just understand that you *will* reap what you sew, so try to allow some time for reflection before making any decision.

You are now officially accountable for your actions and own every decision from this day forward. You cannot avoid consequences by:

1. claiming ignorance
2. blaming others ...or
3. pointing out others' indiscretions.

This brings us to principle #2...

2
If it's not 100% right, it's wrong.

As a teenager, it's your job (or should we call it avocation) to test the limits of what you can get away with while under your parents' guardianship. Consciously, one becomes cognizant of exactly where the edge of the envelope is, and subconsciously, there is a more secure feeling when the parameters you live under are well-defined.

Flash forward. You reach college or a career path, the reins come off, and now it's time to start setting your own boundaries. Hopefully, life experience has given you a good foundation to build upon, but there will be subtle shades of gray thrown into the decision-making process.

If a decision is not 100% right, it's wrong. Let this principle be your litmus test. If every action has a consequence, one must evaluate the pros and the cons – not only for you, but for *anyone* your actions may affect.

The Rotary Four Way Test is a great tool to use as well:
1. Is it the truth?
2. Is it fair to all concerned?
3. Will it build goodwill and better friendships?
4. Will it be beneficial to all concerned?

3

It's none of your business what other people think of you.

Now read that again – slowly. Does it make sense yet? Let me count the ways.

When we grow up we always looked to our parents for guidance and for feedback. And why not? They had our best interest at heart. As teenagers and young adults there is still that urge to get constant feedback from a teacher, a friend, or the random person we empower to fulfill us.

It's none of your business what other people think of you. *It's only your business how you view them.* This particular principle does not discount the two previous chapters – we should still live benevolently – but we can't live to please others. We have to live our own unique life.

Anais Nin once said, "We don't see things as they are, we see them as we are." There is no such thing as an opinion without some form of bias. Don't give an opinion unless solicited, and don't ask for one unless it is from a trusted source.

4

People don't think about you anyway.

I really have to laugh about this particular principle as I begin my 5th decade of existence. I remember in my high school and college years living that hypothetical existence. *What if ABC happened? What will Suzie Cutie think about XYZ? When the hell will I get rid of these zits? What will people think if...?*

When we're younger we are so self-absorbed and evaluate every event that happens (or may happen) in terms of its affect on us. *Everything* is a big deal.

But here is the good news. Nobody cares. Why? Because they are knee deep in their *own* problems, concerns, crises. When you take a breath, rise above your concerns, and look around, the whole world is affected by the same condition.

It took me three years of therapy to learn that one. Skip that trip to the therapists' couch and cut yourself some slack.

5
96% of the things you worry about don't exist

Just to dovetail off the previous chapter, too often we worry about things that should have little to no impact on our daily lives. Negativity can be epidemic and should not be given free rent on the brain. That's snatching defeat from the jaws of victory.

We live in the present and the future has yet to happen. We have no control over anyone else's feelings *or* their actions. Likewise, we can't control the weather, traffic, plants, animals, the Earth, the sun, etc. When you think about it, there is not much we have total control over except our point of view.

I'm not advocating tuning out the world; I'm just begging the question, "Where should our focus be?" To borrow the Twelve Step idiom, if I am "powerless" over people, places, and things, I can't get bent out of shape over people, places, and things.

If we gain some perspective, then the world shrinks a little bit and unexpected problems become manageable. When Murphy's Law rears its ugly head, shrug your shoulders and go on. Focus on what you *can* control – what you *can* do or prepare for. Nobody gets out of this life alive. Don't waste time worrying about what's out of your hands.

6
Friends should edify.
Do yours?

Briefly review your significant relationships (other than your immediate family of course). How many good friends do you have? I mean truly good friends.

What defines a good friend? A good friend stands by you in good times and in bad. Friends can be brutally honest. They will watch your back when you're not around. They want what's best for you.

What actions or traits should raise a red flag? Pettiness? Envy? Jealousy? A friend would not offer you drugs, or ask you to commit a crime (no matter how harmless it may appear). Friends don't steal – literally *or* figuratively. A friend won't desert you in a time of need, or place you in position to be harmed.

This principle should be learned in kindergarten, but is crucial at this point in your life. You are developing relationships now that will shape you as a person and hopefully last a lifetime. Do you believe that you can spend time with someone and not have any of their habits and behaviors rub off on you?

Be discriminating to those you allow into your inner sanctum.

7

You can be right or you can be happy. Not both.

I had to learn this one the hard way, so I hope and pray you take this admonition to heart. Friendships have been lost, marriages have been destroyed, and wars have broken out because one or both parties in an argument had to be right.

Stubbornness is an interesting animal and oftentimes can neither be swayed by facts n*or* common sense. Stubbornness stems from pride, but we'll expand on pride in a succeeding chapter. When talking about relationships, there is a question to be asked. Is it worth destroying the relationship just to prove a point? You may, in fact, be on the correct side of your argument, but always allow the other party some wiggle room.

I'd rather be happy, but if you choose the former, be prepared to dine alone – often.

8.

If you get in a rut, don't move in furniture.

Life is so unpredictable. Sometimes you feel like you're the dog and other times the hydrant. It's a dog-eat-dog world and somehow we get stuck with the milk bone underwear. Life only stops changing when you stop breathing for good.

Like economic cycles, there will be down times. Don't take it personally, and don't stay there. We are not terminally unique in our experiences although we sometimes feel that way. When looking back on your life with that 20/20 hindsight, you'll find that your past failures were the best learning experiences from which to build on.

Failure is an event – not a character trait. Don't become emotionally attached to that event. Accept it, evaluate it, process it, and then dump it. It is our *reaction* to the challenges in life which will define our character.

9.

Self-esteem is vital.
Pride is fatal.

All too often people confuse pride with self-esteem. What's the difference?

Self-esteem is confidence and self-satisfaction. It comes from within. People with self-esteem are comfortable in their own skin and seek to fulfill their own needs while still being considerate of others. They are usually happy and upbeat, and are secure enough to accept criticism or admit when they are wrong. Esteem is a vital human need.

Pride is the polar opposite of self-esteem. A prideful person is not comfortable in his own skin, and only takes pleasure in external things (i.e. status, possessions, etc.). Prideful people constantly compare themselves with other people in an attempt to feel better about themselves. They degrade others constantly and are more concerned with *who* is right rather than *what* is right

Pride is actually a sign of low self-esteem because it is usually a tool to cover insecurity and low self-opinion.

Don't compare how you feel inside with how other people appear outside. False pride only breeds resentment and unhappiness. Learn to value who you are and help others value themselves. If you place a small value upon yourself, be assured that the world won't try to raise your price.

10.

The Joneses won't cry
at your funeral.

I read a funny statistic one time. The number of people who will cry at your funeral can be counted on one hand. So what, right?

The sad part of this truth is that a good portion of the working population in the USA will drive *more* car, buy *more* house, and accumulate *more* stuff to impress people who don't know they exist – *and won't cry at their funeral* (See Chapter 9).

This "stuffitis" in the USA is becoming epidemic. We are increasingly bombarded with advertising which creates dissonance or conflict that can only be exorcised by four easy payments. Understand the game and don't fall into the trap.

Get your feedback from the people who matter to you and truly have your best interest at heart. Spend your time working on and enjoying those relationships.

Just because the Joneses are spending their way into oblivion, doesn't mean you have to. Can't you hear that faint voice of mom speaking right now, *"If everyone jumped off the cliff, would you jump too?"* I hate to tell this to you, but mom was right.

11

Be a good partner to find a good partner.

The dating game can be a rollercoaster ride, because the rules seem to keep changing by the moment. Traditional courtship is passé, and physical and emotional intimacy is often rushed prematurely.

If you ask anyone what they are looking for in a mate, no doubt you will receive a laundry list of desired traits. If that question is posed in reverse, however, and those same people must list what they will be willing to be or to do as a mate, that list is a lot shorter.

To be completely candid, we've selfishly turned dating (for lack of a better word) into a merit/demerit system. We try each other on to see if they fit rather than go through the steps to intimacy.

Are you willing to *be* a good partner? 50% of marriages fail because one or both parties aren't. Remember, love is an action not a destination; and marriage is a commitment, not a trial period.

Here's another great morsel. If you always seem to have the "unhealthy" relationships, look in the mirror. Healthy people don't date sick people and vice versa. You've got to fix *you* before the desirable ones will appear.

12
Save 10%.

My grandfather drilled this little gem into my mind at a fairly young age, but unfortunately I didn't start saving aggressively until *after* age 30.

I'm trying to remain politically neutral because this a hot button issue, but I *was* an economics major. *You can retire a millionaire no matter the rate of income you are paid, by saving 10%.* The earlier you start, of course, the earlier you can retire.

The law of compound interest is real – the math doesn't lie. A person who starts out making minimum wage can retire a millionaire if she starts saving at a young age, and a person who makes $1 million per year can die broke without a savings plan.

A 21 year old person who starts investing $1500 per year can retire at age 65 with $1.076 million at 10% interest. The stock market has yielded a return of 11-12% over the last century, and even the most conservative investing will yield well enough to retire at a decent age.

Fiscal discipline is best learned early. Living on less than you make is not a sacrifice, it's necessary. Deferred gratification is a virtue. Hold true to this principle and you will go far.

BUSINESS

13
Find what you're passionate about and *Do It.*

At first glance this principle is rather elementary, but should definitely not be discounted. Spend some time journaling and/or taking some assessment tests in order to see where your temperament and skills may lead you. Stretch yourself in your course work; get creative and expose yourself to the new and different.

Here are some tips:

1. Don't live for mom and dad. If you live for someone else, there will always be resentment and disappointment in the end. Ask their advice but *you* decide your own life. Believe me; they'll still invite you for Thanksgiving dinner.
2. Don't necessarily fall for the "hot job" that everyone else seems to be applying for. What's hot today could be gone tomorrow.
3. Ask yourself the question that if money weren't an obstacle, what would you rather be doing at this very moment? The answer will give you insight into where your focus should be.
4. Less than 30% of people work in the same field as their major. Don't limit your opportunities.

14

You owe your employer
your best effort – always.

I've listed this principle under the business category, but it should really be universally applied. Every one of us has had a job that they didn't like, or perhaps, we've worked somewhere and felt we weren't being adequately paid for our efforts.

Think of your employment as a contract between yourself and your boss. Your hours and rate of pay have been decided in advance, so the minute you step foot in the workplace, that contract is binding.

Places of business are not Utopian environments. You will find coworkers who don't want to be there, supervisors who are overbearing or detached, and millions of other reasons to withhold your best effort.

Give maximum effort at all times. You are not only representing your employer, you are representing yourself, and creating habits that will be difficult to break. But most of all, refusing to give your best effort is a form of theft. It's stealing.

You can never escape shoddy work or insufficient effort. It will follow you everywhere you go. Why? Because *you're* everywhere you go, and those memories will follow you.

Be that person who can look back fondly and say, "You know, that was a tough job but I'm glad I gave it all I had." Plus, one never knows when a recommendation from an old employer is the key to the perfect job. Don't burn bridges.

15
Take a sales course.

Some of us actually will go into sales as a career, but most of us won't. However, the skills learned by taking a sales training course will translate into any profession. Unfortunately, the average citizen envisions a salesperson as the telemarketer who interrupts dinner or the door to door vacuum salesman who won't take no for an answer. Relationship or needs-based selling has become the new paradigm. Here are some skills that can be discerned.

To start, everyone needs an elevator speech (i.e. the ability to tell who you are and what you do in twenty seconds or less). Putting your thoughts into a concise format is always a good practice.

Secondly, the ability to ask open-ended questions (questions that cannot be answered with a yes or no) will take you far. Information is a precious commodity, and getting people to open up and talk about themselves is invaluable. Think of the possibilities for social situations, graduate school, job interviews, etc.

Thirdly, there will be numerous times in life where you will have to "sell" your idea or point of view. Properly assessing what your audience is looking for, positioning your proposition in the best light, and triggering the desired response, are necessary skills.

Lastly, everyone "buys" a product, a service, or a thought, for *emotional* reasons; but will look to affirm that decision by *logical* ones. Learn the psychology behind decision-making, and you will be miles ahead.

16
When problem solving, start from where you are.

I love to race sailboats, and during the off-season will often read up on tactics and strategies from the experts. David Dellenbaugh, a famous Americas Cup tactician and helmsman, wrote in one of his columns that the key to getting back in a race is to *start from where you are.*

In fleet racing very rarely can you get the very best start, and sometimes wind conditions or other boats will put you behind or on the wrong side of a race course. The "old" sailor in me would get frustrated or try some risky move to gain back all that I had lost, much to my detriment.

What Dellenbaugh is saying is that you have to erase everything that happened up to this point in time. This is my new reality. What is the first thing I need to do, second thing I need to do, etc.?

In business we can get so caught up in past decisions made by management or ourselves that it causes inaction in the here and now. The worst thing you can do in a situation is to replay the old events. You can't fix the past, and the future is being determined right now. Assess your current reality, adjust or develop your strategy to it, and sail on.

17
Think like an Entrepreneur

This principle is all about the big picture. Whether you own your own business, work for a small company, work for a large company, become a homemaker or a teacher; thinking like an entrepreneur is vital. *You* are your own business. Thinking in this way is empowering.

As an entrepreneur we are constantly working *on* our "business" – building better systems, more effective service delivery, developing long range goals, strategic plans, etc. All of these efforts, of course, are performed with the customer(s) in mind.

As an entrepreneur, all of the tasks in my organization must be defined and delegated to the proper personnel. If I am a sole proprietor, chances are that all or most of the tasks will be mine, but they must still be clearly defined and ready to be handed off as my business grows. If I am in middle management or the frontline, my customers may be my employees or upper management.

Build a long range plan (10 to 20 years) toward your "preferred reality" and work backwards until you reach specific immediate tasks. This process will initially take some time, but you will gain focus, drive, and bring responsibility and accountability into your organization.

18
Learn to enjoy the success of others.

Business and professional success is not a solo effort. Many times we will view the success of our peers as a threat to our own advancement rather than an achievement for our organization. Our own insecurity may cause us to withhold support or even sabotage the effort of our own teammates.

True leaders help others shine. They get to know the people around them, praise them often when warranted, and are quick to come to the aid of their peers. These traits are even more vital when in a supervisory capacity. Dissatisfaction with an immediate supervisor is one of the main reasons people change jobs or refuse to give full effort. Over $400 billion production per year is lost due to employee disengagement.

Human beings have a psychological need to be accepted and respected. A person will perform at a higher level in order to validate a compliment. If we edify others in our words and actions, they will feel valued, and will eagerly try to live up to the reputation that you have set out for them.

Make yourself a leader within your organization, and you will become indispensable.

19
Life is straight commission.

There once was a time (in a galaxy not too far away) that men and women worked for the same company most of their adult lives. That doesn't happen anymore. Twenty years ago the average person worked for 5 companies before retiring. That number has doubled today and doesn't look to be shrinking any time soon.

This fact frightens a lot of people but it shouldn't. Don't go complaining to your congressman or take over the school administration building complaining about fairness. Market forces are at work, and labor (just like capital) should be free to flow to its highest and best use.

We determine our own worth in the marketplace. Being raised in an entitlement generation, this principle is unfortunately lost on many people. *We* determine our education level, our skill level, and our income level. Yes, our income level.

You will make as much or a little as you feel comfortable making. It has been proven empirically that the average American will adjust his living standards down to an income level instead of performing the behaviors (or taking the risks) necessary to achieve a higher or desired income. In other words, the 5%-10% who *will* perform those necessary behaviors will achieve their desired income levels

Anyone can be an entrepreneur if they so choose – though most choose not to. We are empowered to choose what suits our temperament and our abilities. Each person must understand that we alone are responsible and accountable for our own choices.

20

If you live in the USA – you're half way to success already.

We've reached that point in the book where I get out my flag and start waving. Our country is the most incredible country in the world. We invented the middle class and have been an incredible beta test for multi-cultural democracy. No other country is more altruistic. No other country has had the economic growth.

America is not perfect, but don't concentrate on the warts instead of viewing the body as a whole. There *is* no better place to achieve success than right here in the U.S. of A. – no matter your nationality, sex, or age. For every story of oppression you hear, I can name ten stories of success.

Unfortunately, the free enterprise system has its detractors – those who focus on its abuses. However, we can't dump the baby out with the bath water. I'd rather be hurt by too much liberty than handcuffed by too little.

The free market system is the country's engine, and allows anyone from anywhere to grab a slice of the American dream. It's our responsibility to celebrate and cherish and carve *our* slice of the dream. And don't forget the whipped cream.

Recommended Reading

- Dale Carnegie – <u>How to Win Friends and Influence People</u> (still the gold standard)
- Michael E. Gerber – <u>The E Myth Revisited</u> (An eye-opener)
- Kurt Mortensen – <u>Maximum Influence</u> (tremendous insight into why we behave like we do)
- Tim Sanders – <u>Love is the Killer App</u> (the new networking paradigm)
- Jim Collins – <u>Good to Great</u> (how the best companies became that way)
- Jack Canfield, Mark Victor Hansen, et. al. <u>Chicken Soup for the Soul</u> (I'm sure they have one for every career path now)
- Steven R. Covey – <u>7 Habits of Highly Effective People</u> (another must read)
- John C. Maxwell – <u>The 360 Degree Leader</u> (leading from where you are)
- John Gray - <u>Men Are From Mars, Women Are From Venus</u> (Dating 101)
- Neal Boortz, John Linder – <u>The Fair Tax Book</u> (responsibility in government)
- <u>The Bible</u> (good action, solid applications, great ending)

About the Author

Kurt McDowell is a graduate of Brown University and the school of hard knocks. He currently manages *McDowell Incentives, Inc.*, an employee performance improvement company and resides in Oklahoma City with his wife and two children.

www.ingramcontent.com/pod-product-compliance
Lightning Source LLC
Chambersburg PA
CBHW031327290526
45784CB00014B/2399